D0816004

KENDRA PETERSON
DRIZZLE KITCHEN FAVORITES
happy foods for every body and every allergy

Completely customizable recipes with allergy friendly substitutions for any ingredient considered part of the Top-8 food allergens.

This publication contains the opinions and ideas of its author. It is intended to provide helpful and informative material on the subjects addressed in the publication. It is sold with the understanding that the author and publisher are not engaged in rendering medical, health or any other kind of personal professional services in this book. The reader should consult his or her medical, health, or other competent professional before adopting any of the suggestions in this book or drawing inferences from it.

The author and publisher specifically disclaim all responsibility for any liability, loss or risk, personal or otherwise, which is incurred as a consequence, directly or indirectly, of the use and application of any of the contents of this book.

Cover photography by Greg Byers, www.gregorybyersstudio.com
Book design and production by Sydney Wippman, sydneywippman.com
Food photography by Marcin Cymmer, www.smartpixelstudio.com
All photography copyright @2017 Kendra Peterson

Copyright @2017 by Kendra Peterson
All rights reserved. This book and any portion thereof may not be reproduced or used in any manner whatsoever without the express written permission of the publisher except for the use of brief quotations in a book review.

Printed in the United States of America

First Printing, 2017

ISBN-13: 978-0692990018
ISBN-10: 069299001

Happy Foods Alchemy
1222 W. Madison Street
#423
Chicago IL 60607

drizzlekitchen.com

Mom, you passed when I was so young
I often have a hard time remembering you.
But when I cook I feel you with me. You
taught me the importance of good food,
the magic of a proper dinner and gave me the
gift of the kitchen. This book is for you.

INDEX

Introduction

Happy Breakfasts

Happy Lunches

Happy Sides

INDEX

KENDRA'S STORY

Why are these recipes happy? Because I am a happy chef!

As a little girl in the kitchen, I'd watch my mother put loving attention into our meals, to our holidays, to the table setting and to the food. She specialized in entertaining with ease and presenting the most elaborate of Julia Child's recipes. It all seemed like a magic. I wanted to someday create that for myself, that elegance and beauty she drizzled through the kitchen.

I lost my mother when I was 8. I began cooking then, and I never stopped. Her love and passion for food remain in my blood and bones. It started with simple recipes. By the time high school arrived, I was inviting friends over after school for hand-rolled pasta and freshly whipped chocolate mousse. I loved seeing everyone enjoying the food that I enjoyed preparing.

When I got to university, it seemed natural to study food science and nutrition. While I loved it, the classic path of registered dietitian wasn't mine. So right after college, I wore many hats. I ran culinary programs and opened up stores for Williams-Sonoma. I taught myself how to make wedding cakes and custom cookies, running a little business out of my apartment. I taught cooking classes at a school in downtown Chicago.

Then my first Drizzle Kitchen private chef client landed in my lap...then my second...then my third. Before I knew it, I had a brand. I provided weekly meals prepared in my clients' homes, completely customized to their preferences and allergies. I used the knowledge about food that I learned in school to care for people through food as I learned from my mother.

My focus clarified after one particular client. I met the family initially to prepare food for just one of their children, to help manage challenging behavioral issues, and in the process we transformed the entire family's food lifestyle.

Nobody was eating together. The parent who had been making most meals felt overwhelmed by food sensitivities and understanding safe foods. They needed food happiness. They needed the joy that food and family meal time brought them. After some time, cooking classes and family eating became a regular thing. Even the kids planned meals that everyone ate. The shift in the family dynamic was remarkable. Knowing that I had a part in that shifted my focus, too. After that experience, I wanted to work with people who needed more than just nutritious meals. They needed special meals for a specific reason. They needed to find their joy and safety in food again.

Today, I have a happy and bustling business. I have wonderful chefs and food lovers who work with me. I adore every single one of my clients. We work with families dealing with cancer, debilitating diagnoses and life threatening allergies. We work with professional athletes focused on honing performance and celebrities shifting their diet for acting roles. We prepare meals, travel with clients and deliver food to hospitals.

Every single one of our clients finds us because they see food as a challenge, eating as exhausting, and nutritional knowledge as overwhelming. My purpose is to help them find a better way with food. Often our clients spend time in the kitchen with me, asking questions about ingredients and methods. They engage and enjoy conversations about food again. I help them fall in love with food- again or for the first time ever.

As a chef I bring my own happiness and joy into the food I prepare for my clients. I believe when you are happy, your food tastes better. And when your food truly provides what you need, you are happier. So, let's get to it! Xo~ Kendra

THE DRIZZLE KITCHEN HAPPY FOOD LIFE

Part of the joy of cooking is becoming a Happy Foods Alchemist! This book gives you the resources to create your own versions of recipes and meals. Whether it be a food allergy or a preference ingredient substitutions are provided for you to customize within all the Top-8 Food allergens to be safe and happy recipes just for you!

Consider my recipes your template.

Get creative! If you don't like cilantro, add parsley! If you don't like quinoa, try adding brown rice or millet! A recipe, and a meal, is most enjoyable when you indulge in creative freedom. So make the recipes as directed once or twice (and don't forget that, "t" means teaspoon and "T" means Tablespoon!). Then have fun! Add your own spin and make them your own.

Then, get to seasoning.

These recipes provide some guidance on adding salt, fats and acid at the end. ("Fats" means any oils or butter and "acid" is just a fancy term for vinegar or citrus.) Any of these can amp up your recipe with just the slightest amount added. You'll notice in my recipes that I don't add a bunch of salt- and sometimes I don't list any. With baking, you must be precise and measured. But with cooking, you have the freedom to add as your palate likes. So, if you add a pinch of salt while cooking but find you still need more, then add more! Likewise, if you make something and think, "Well, this needs a little something extra," but aren't sure what, try a squeeze of lemon or a little drizzle of apple cider vinegar. Take cooking into your own hands and be confident! You've got this.

Remember, nutrition is about more than food.

Water and sleep are two things that affect your food life that many people forget about. Often when you think you're hungry, it's actually thirst that you need to quench. And I think we all know how much better we feed ourselves when we get proper sleep. Lack of sleep and the morning sprint out the door makes donuts at the coffee shop look that much better! So drink plenty of water (maybe throw some lemons and limes in there!) and get yourself at least 7 hours of sleep. I promise you'll be happier, healthier and you'll eat better!

And, always, eat with joy.

The most important gift you can give yourself is to eat with joy. Think about how much better food tastes when you are out to dinner with your friends or at a beautiful holiday dinner with your family. Food made with love and eaten with joy just tastes better. Now science is proving that eating with happiness improves nutritious food choices.

Allow yourself to slow down for a second. Cook with friends, cook with family, drink water, get enough sleep and share some really great meals.

Happy Eating, Friends!

KENDRA'S FAVORITE FRITTATA

Serves 8

Ingredients
1 pint grape tomatoes
12 eggs*
2 small sweet potatoes, scrubbed well and diced
1 shallot, chopped
2 cups chopped lacinato kale (sometimes also called dinosaur kale)
¼ c. finely chopped chive
Optional topping: ½ c. grated parmigiano or mozzarella cheese

Directions

1. Preheat oven to 400. Toss the grape tomatoes with a nice glug of olive oil and place on a parchment lined baking sheet. Sprinkle with sea salt and pepper and roast in preheated oven for 20 minutes until slightly browned. Then turn oven down to 325. Meanwhile, gently whisk the eggs until white and yolks are totally blended. Set aside.

2. Preheat a 10" nonstick skillet over medium heat on the stove. Add a glug of olive oil and the diced sweet potatoes. Saute for a few minutes. Then add a little water, cover with lid and allow sweet potatoes to steam. Continue adding the water and covering with lid until the potatoes are cooked through, about 7-8 minutes.

3. Add the chopped shallot and the kale to the pan with the potatoes and gently toss together until the kale is slightly wilted. Remove from the pan onto a plate.

4. Add another small glug of olive oil to the empty nonstick pan, turn the heat down to low and pour in the whisked eggs.

5. Add the reserved sautéed vegetables in an even layer and then top with the roasted grape tomatoes. Cook on the stove until the outside begins to set, about 10-15 minutes. Then, sprinkle the top with cheese, if using, and finish with the chives.

6. Place pan into the 325 degree oven and bake until the center is cooked through, another 10-15 minutes (it shouldn't be wobbly anymore but you also don't want it too browned!).

7. Gently slide onto a cutting board and cool a few minutes. Then slice and enjoy! This will keep very well in the fridge for 3-4 days. Reheat wedges wrapped in foil at 350 for 13-14 minutes or heat the entire frittata at 350 for 20-25 minutes on a tray, lightly tented with foil.

*TO MAKE EGG FREE: Roast and saute the vegetables as noted in the recipe above. Instead of sprinkling the vegetables onto eggs, prepare a chickpea flour crust instead: Whisk together 1 1/4 c. chickpea flour with 1/2 c. water, 3 T. olive oil, 1 t. salt and 1 t. garlic powder. Preheat a nonstick pan and a plug of olive oil. Pour the chickpea flour mixture into the pan and cook over medium heat for 3-4 minutes until the bottom is just beginning to set. Sprinkle the sauteed vegetables to the top (and any cheese and the chive, if you are using). Place in a 350 degree oven for 10-15 minutes until the chickpea base is set. Remove, slide onto a cutting board and serve!

HAPPY HELPS: You can also use already roasted or cooked sweet potatoes! This is a trick of mine... when I roast veggies for dinner I almost always double the quantity so I can throw them into a salad or a frittata to make for quick cooking!

MACA MATCHA SMOOTHIE

I like to have this smoothie either for breakfast or as a post workout recovery shake! A nutritional powerhouse that provides protein, stress relieving adaptogens and hormone balancing. Healthy fats, fiber, iron and antioxidants are more natural benefits this delicious shake delivers to your belly!

Ingredients
2 c. favorite non-sweetened, dairy free milk
1 frozen banana
2 t. ceremonial matcha
1 t. maca powder
2 scoops collagen powder
4 medjool dates, soaked in warm water and pits removed
2 handfuls of baby spinach
2 T. coconut manna OR ½ avocado
Optional add ins: ashwaganda powder, hemp seeds, cacao nibs, bee pollen

Directions
1. Add all the ingredients into the pitcher of a blender, add a few ice cubs and blend on high speed until smooth and frothy.

2. Pour into two glasses and enjoy!

OVERNIGHT OATS WITH RASPBERRY-DATE JAM

Ingredients
¾ c. old fashioned, gluten free oats
3 cups coconut milk, or your favorite dairy free milk
1/3 c. chia seeds
½ t. vanilla
½ t. ground cinnamon
Raspberry-date jam
1 cup frozen raspberries with juice
4 medjool dates, pitted and chopped
Optional toppings
¼ c. sunflower seed butter
¼ T. hemp seeds
¼ c. toasted coconut

Directions
1. In a bowl mix together the oats, coconut milk, chia seeds, vanilla and ground cinnamon. Whisk well and let sit for 10-15 minutes.

2. Meanwhile make the raspberry date jam by warming together the raspberries and chopped medjool dates in a small saucepan for 5-6 minutes. Turn off the heat and let sit for another 10 minutes.

3. Divide the oat mixture and liquid equally into 4 mason jars. Top with the raspberry-date jam and then the sunflower seed butter, hemp seeds and toasted coconut.

4. Place in the refrigerator to fully thicken and enjoy a delightful breakfast the next morning!

9

QUINOA BREAKFAST PIZZA

Ingredients
Topping
1 pint grape tomatoes, halved
2 cups arugula or spinach, chopped
6 eggs*
1 cup grated mozzarella cheese**
¼ c. sliced fresh basil
olive oil
salt
Crust
2 cups cooked quinoa
3 egg whites, whisked*
1 T. dried oregano
2 T. grated parmesan cheese**
½ t. salt

Directions
1. Preheat oven to 425. Toss the halved grape tomatoes with a little glug of olive oil and a sprinkle of sea salt. Pour into a parchment paper lined rimmed baking sheet and roast for 20-25 minutes until lightly browned.

2. Meanwhile, stir together all the crust ingredients in a bowl. Heat a 10-inch nonstick fry pan over medium heat and add a glug of oil. Pour the quinoa mixture into the preheated pan and press out with the back of a spoon, pressing a little higher around the edges to create a crust.

3. Cook on the stove for 5-6 minutes until barely set.

4. Turn oven down to 350 and then place the nonstick pan with the quinoa crust inside. Cook for 10 minutes or until the quinoa is no longer wet and feels firm to the touch.

5. Sprinkle the chopped arugula or spinach all over the crust and create little "nests" for the eggs to fit into. Crack eggs into these little "nests" and sprinkle the roasted tomatoes around.

6. Place back in the oven for another 10-15 minutes until the egg yolks are just set. Remove from the oven and sprinkle with the mozzarella. Bake another 5 minutes until cheese is just melted. Top with basil and a little salt. Cut into 8 slices and enjoy!

*TO MAKE EGG FREE: Prepare crust with 2 c. cooked quinoa+¼ c. hot water+½ c. almond flour OR gluten free all purpose flour +1 T. olive oil. Mix together with your hands and press into a parchment lined 9" cake pan. Follow remaining instructions, eliminating the nested egg in instruction #5.

**TO MAKE DAIRY FREE: Replace with your favorite dairy free cheese, add a pinch of nutritional yeast or simply eliminate!

HAPPY HELPS: This reheats very well through the course of the week as a great grab and go breakfast. Wrap the cut slices individually in foil and store. Warm each slice at 350 for 10 minutes until heated through and enjoy!

TROPICAL GREENS SMOOTHIE

This is one of my favorite ways to start the day. I make this smoothie weekly for one family I work with. I made a spicy version for the dad and a non spicy version for the kids, package them individually in mason jars and they all have a jar on the way to work and school.

Ingredients
1 bag frozen, organic mango
1 bag frozen, organic pineapple
½ c. packed cilantro
½ bag frozen chopped kale or 2 cups packed spinach
4" slice cucumber
1/3 c. chopped frozen broccoli
2 whole oranges, peeled
zest and juice from 2 limes
2 scoops powdered collagen

Directions
1. Place everything in a blender and puree until everything is super smooth.

2. Pour into Mason jars and enjoy right away or keep in the refrigerator for 2-3 days to enjoy greens on the go!

ENERGIZER BUNNY QUINOA SALAD

This quinoa has a great combination of flavors and also nutrition; plenty of protein, carbohydrates, vitamins and minerals from vegetables to keep you satisfied and nourished! On a weekly basis I prepare this salad for one of my clients who is a surgeon. It keeps him energized and nourished while in the operating room~

Ingredients
2 cups cooked, shredded chicken breast
2 cups cooked quinoa
1 cup baby arugula
1 cup shelled baby lima beans (or edamame or peas)
handful of green grapes, halved
½ cup chopped cilantro
½ cup chopped mint leaves
½ c. marcona almonds or toasted sunflower seeds
Dressing
zest and juice from 2 limes
1/3 c. olive oil
1 serrano pepper
1 clove garlic, peeled
1 T. honey
¼ cup chopped cilantro stems
sprinkle of sea salt

Directions
1. In a large bowl combine the shredded chicken, cooked quinoa, baby arugula, baby lima beans, halved grapes, cilantro, mint and marcona almonds.

2. Prepare the dressing by popping all the ingredients in a blender and blend until well mixed. Taste for seasoning and adjust with more honey or more salt as needed.

3. Pour over the quinoa and mix until well combined.

4. This salad lasts well in the refrigerator for 4–5 days.

Happy Helps: Here's how I roast my chicken for salads! Preheat oven to 425. Line a small rimmed baking sheet with parchment paper and place bone in, skin on chicken breasts on top. Drizzle lightly with olive oil and sprinkle with sea salt. Roast for 40 minutes or until golden brown and fully cooked. Cool and shred.

15

KALE & SWEET POTATO SALAD
WITH TAHINI-MAPLE DRESSING

Ingredients
2 sweet potatoes, scrubbed well and diced
1 bunch lacinato kale, stems stripped
1 cup shelled edamame*
2 T. hemp seeds
2 T. toasted sunflower seeds
2 T. toasted pumpkin seeds
coconut oil or olive oil
sea salt
Dressing
3 T. tahini paste
2 T. water
3 T. olive oil
juice from 1 lemon
1 garlic clove, peeled
1-2 t. maple syrup, depending on your preference for sweet!
sea salt

Directions
1. Preheat the oven to 400, convection if you have that option. Line a baking sheet with parchment paper.

2. Toss the sweet potatoes with either some coconut oil or olive oil and spread out on the parchment lined baking sheet. Sprinkle with a little sea salt and pop in the oven.

3. Roast potatoes for 20-30 minutes until lightly browned. Remove and cool.

4. Finely chop the lacinato kale and toss into a bowl. Add the cooled potatoes, shelled edamame, hemp seeds, sunflower seeds and pumpkin seeds.

5. To make the dressing pop all the ingredients in a blender and blend together until creamy and frothy. Add more maple syrup if you'd like it a little sweeter and feel free to add more water to reach the consistency you would like. I like mine pretty thick!

6. Pour the dressing over the bowl of vegetables, toss to coat and enjoy! This salad also keeps well for 2-3 days so it's great to make for a few lunches through the week.

*TO MAKE SOY FREE: Substitute baby lima beans or sweet peas for the edamame.

RED LENTIL AND COCONUT SOUP

Ingredients

1 bunch green onions, chopped
3" chunk ginger, peeled and finely minced
3 cloves garlic, finely minced
¼ c. chopped cilantro stems (it's a great way to use a part that's usually tossed away!)
½ pound shiitake mushrooms, stems removed and caps sliced
1 stalk lemongrass, peeled and the center chopped
1 carrot, diced
1 sweet potato, scrubbed well and diced
1 red pepper, diced
1 c. red lentils, sorted through for stones
1 can full fat coconut milk*
2 c. mushroom or vegetable broth
2 heads baby bok choy, sliced
juice from 1 lime
½ c. chopped cilantro
coconut oil or vegetable oil, for cooking

Directions

1. Preheat a soup pot over medium heat. Add a spoonful of coconut or vegetable oil and then the chopped green onions, minced ginger, minced garlic, chopped cilantro stems and sliced shiitake caps. Stir until fragrant, 3-4 minutes.

2. Add the lemongrass, carrot and the diced sweet potato along with another scoop of coconut oil and saute for 3-4 minutes until the sweet potatoes and carrots are just beginning to soften.

3. Add the diced red pepper, the red lentils, the coconut milk, the broth and stir. Bring to a boil then turn down to a simmer and cover.

4. Simmer for 20 minutes or until the lentils have softened.

5. Taste for seasoning and add more salt as needed.

6. Add the sliced bok choy and stir for a few minutes until the bok choy is softened.

7. Just before serving add the lime juice and the chopped cilantro.

*TO MAKE TREE NUT FREE: Add 1 c. more vegetable broth in lieu of coconut milk.

GRILLED VEGGIE & HALLOUMI SALAD
WITH CHARRED ONION DRESSNG

I first made this salad when I travelled with one of my clients to their beautiful summer home in upper Michigan. We went to the farmers market and grabbed anything that looked fresh and gorgeous, so pretty much everything! It's such a simple salad but so flavorful and has now become a favorite among many of my clients.

Ingredients
1 zucchini, halved lengthwise
1 yellow squash, halved lengthwise
1 red pepper, cored and halved
1 bunch asparagus, ends trimmed
1 bunch green onions, ends trimmed
8 oz. halloumi or other "grilling" cheese*
1 t. smoky paprika
1/3 cup olive oil
3 T. sherry vinegar
½ cup cilantro, chopped
salt and pepper

Directions
1. Preheat a grill to about 400. Clean grates and then oil lightly.

2. While the grill is warming toss the prepared zucchini, yellow squash, red pepper, asparagus and green onions with some olive oil and salt. Place on a tray.

3. Pat the outside of the halloumi dry with paper towels. Then brush the outside of the cheese with olive oil. Place on the tray with the prepared vegetables.

4. Grill the vegetables over high heat for just a few minutes, until they are cooked but still slightly crisp. Turn heat down to low and oil the grates again.

5. Grill the halloumi for about 3-4 minutes per side. It should be nicely golden brown and crispy on both sides, should easily release when slowly lifted.

6. To make the dressing take half of the grilled green onions and mince them. Place in the pitcher of a blender. Add the smoky paprika, the olive oil, sherry vinegar and a pinch of salt and crack of pepper. Blend until all combined.

7. Cut the grilled vegetables, including the remaining green onions, into 1-2" chunks and place in a bowl. Cut the grilled halloumi into 1" cubes and throw in with the vegetables. Pour the dressing over the top and toss to combine. Scoop onto serving platter and sprinkle with the cilantro. Serve at room temperature.

*TO MAKE DAIRY FREE: Use your favorite allergy friendly cheese, diced but not grilled (it will warm from the heat of the vegetables) or deeply saute some mushrooms for a similar umami factor that the cheese would provide!

ALL PURPOSE SALAD TOPPER

Ingredients
¾ c. hemp seeds
¾ c. toasted pumpkin seeds (Austrian pumpkin seeds if you can find them!)
½ c. nutritional yeast
1 T. garlic powder
1 T. sea salt
Optional add ins: ashwaganda powder, reishi powder, chia seeds

Directions
1. Pour all the ingredients in the bowl of a small food processor. Pulse until they have combined and the pumpkin seeds have been slightly chopped.

2. Pour into a glass jar and enjoy for 2-3 weeks on your salads or even over soups! Store in the refrigerator to last a bit longer.

COCONUT WHIPPED BUTTERNUT SQUASH

Ingredients
1- 3 lb. butternut squash
3 T. coconut cream*
1 T. coconut oil**
1-2 T. maple syrup
salt, to taste

Directions
1. Preheat oven to 375.

2. Slice off the stem end of the squash and then very carefully cut in half lengthwise from the top to the bottom.

3. Rub a little coconut oil over the cut side of the squash and place that side down onto a parchment lined baking sheet.

4. Roast until liquid has started to leach out and the squash is super tender when a knife is pierced through the skin.

5. Scoop out seeds and discard. Scoop flesh into the bowl of a food processor and puree until fairly smooth. Pour into a fine mesh sieve set over a bowl and strain out the excess water for about 20 minutes.

6. Pour back into the bowl of the food processor and add the coconut cream, coconutoil, 1 T. of the maple syrup and a sprinkle of salt. Blend until super smooth and creamy. Add more maple syrup or salt to your taste. Enjoy!

*TO MAKE TREE NUT FREE: You can eliminate the coconut cream entirely or use any "cream" substitute suitable for your allergies!
**Instead of coconut oil, you can use butter, ghee, vegan "butter" or allergy free butter.

PARMESAN CRUSTED POTATOES

A favorite among every single one of my clients, these potatoes are so easy to make and delicious with a variety of entrees!

Ingredients
1 lb. smallest yellow potatoes or fingerlings
olive oil
sea salt
½ cup grated parmesan cheese (the real stuff….none of that shelf stable plastic bottle nonsense!)*

Directions
1. Preheat oven to 375 and line a rimmed baking sheet with parchment paper.

2. Cut potatoes into even sized chunks, preferably simply in half. Toss with olive oil and sea salt. Pour onto sheet tray.

3. Flip potatoes so the cut side is on the baking sheet.

4. Roast until tender, about 20 minutes.

5. Remove from the oven and use the back of a fork to press the potatoes gently so they still stay in form but are a little flattened.

6. Drizzle with a tiny bit more olive oil and then sprinkle the parmesan evenly over all the potatoes.

7. Bake until cheese is melted for gooey potatoes, about 5 minutes, or leave in or leave in 10-15 minutes for crispier potatoes.

*TO MAKE DAIRY FREE: You can also simply eliminate the sprinkling of cheese and instead sprinkle with some garlic powder.

SESAME-MISO ROASTED BROCCOLI

Ingredients

3 heads of broccoli, ends trimmed slightly and cut into florets
Marinade
2 T. toasted sesame oil
2 T. chickpea miso
1 clove of garlic, grated over a microplane
1 T. maple syrup
2 T. tahini
1-2 T. brown rice vinegar
1 T. toasted sesame seeds

Directions

1. Preheat oven to 400. Line a baking sheet with parchment paper and set aside.

2. Mix together all the marinade ingredients with a whisk until you have a thick coating, should be like yogurt. Add more water to thin or more miso/tahini to thicken if needed.

3. Place the broccoli in a large bowl and pour the marinade over. Toss with tongs to coat all of the broccoli. Pour onto prepared baking sheet.

4. Roast at 400 for 22-25 minutes until the broccoli is lightly crisped and brown on top.

CHEESE SAUCE FOR ANYTHING

Ingredients

1 medium head cauliflower, end removed and then cut into large pieces
2-3 cups chicken or vegetable broth
2 T. unsalted butter*
2 cups shredded cheddar cheese**

Directions

1. Place the cauliflower pieces in a saucepan and cover with the broth, ensuring the cauliflower is covered with liquid.

2. Simmer until tender and then, using a slotted spoon, scoop the cauliflower into a high speed blender or food processor but save the cooking liquid!

3. Add the butter and blend until the cauliflower is super creamy and smooth, adding the cooking liquid little by little until it just blends. You want this pretty thick.

4. Add half the cheese and pulse until it is mixed in. Add the remaining cheese and pulse again until cheese is melted, this should happen pretty quickly. Add salt as needed, to taste.

5. Enjoy with your favorite cooked vegetable, use as a cheese sauce to cover chicken, mix into steamed rice or even mix with some pasta or zucchini noodles!

*TO MAKE DAIRY FREE: Use your favorite allergy friendly "butter."
   **Use your favorite allergy friendly cheese shreds or a sprinkle of nutritional yeast plus garlic powder for a vitamin B boost and some vegan umami flavor!

CRISPY ROASTED CAULIFLOWER

Ingredients
1 large or 2 small heads of cauliflower
3 T. olive oil, melted coconut oil or grapeseed oil
sea salt

Directions
1. Preheat the oven to 425, preferably convection if you have that on your oven. Line a rimmed baking sheet with parchment paper.

2. Trim the stalk off the cauliflower and then cut the florets into small pieces. Place in a large bowl and toss with your chosen oil.

3. Pour onto the lined baking sheet and sprinkle with a nice pinch of sea salt.

4. Roast at 425 for 15 minutes, toss and roast for another 10-20 minutes until crispy and golden brown. (If you have a convection oven this will happen faster rather than if you don't.)

BALSAMIC ROSEMARY MARINATED STEAK

This is a timeless marinade that works so well with steak. Hanger steak is one of my favorite cuts because of it's delicious flavor, fat marbling throughout and it's forgiving nature. A very tender and easy cut to work with but if you can't find hanger steak then pick up a nice flank steak and just be sure to marinate overnight!

Ingredients
8 sprigs of rosemary, leaves stripped and finely minced
4 garlic cloves, grated over a microplane or finely minced
¼ c. olive oil
2 T. balsamic vinegar
1 T. maple syrup
1 ½ pounds of hanger steak or skirt steak

Directions
1. Mix together all of the marinde ingredients in a large re-sealable bag.

2. Add the steak and toss to coat. Press as much air out as you can and seal bag. Marinate for 4–24 hours.

3. When ready to cook, remove the steak and pat dry with paper towels. Cook either on a hot grill for a 5–6 minutes per side or under the broiler for 4–5 minutes per side.

4. Let steak rest for 8–10 minutes with foil lightly tented on top. Slice and enjoy!

HAPPY HELPS: It's important to allow steak to rest for 5-10 minutes after cooking it. When you cook steak the moisture all moves toward the very center of the cut, a protective measure. When you slice into it right away after cooking much of that liquid leaches out of the beef and you lose it to your cutting board. If you allow the meat to "rest" for a few minutes, during that time the moisture is all redistributed allowing for less to leach out when you slice it!

MY FAVORITE MISO MARINADE

I love to use this marinade on everything from cod and salmon to chicken thighs to portabello mushrooms. Just be sure to whisk the miso so you have no lumps and let the marinade soak in your meat/fish/veg for at least an hour or up until 24.

Ingredients

1/3 c. chickpea miso
1/3 c. sake
3 T. warmed honey
3 T. mirin
Optional add in: about 1" knob fresh ginger, grated

Directions

1. Whisk everything together and pour over your meat, fish or vegetables. Allow to marinade at least one hour and up until 24.

2. When ready to cook, gently remove from the marinade and shake of excess but don't wipe off. Cook in preferred method (grill, broil, oven).

CHICKEN PARMIGIANA MEATBALLS

These initially came to be as part of an outdoor summer bbq for a client in the fo[...]
burgers! Once grilling season ended I turned them into meatballs. The flavors are [...]
awesome either way so try whichever one sounds best to you!

Ingredients
½ cup sundried tomatoes, not the oil packed
1 pound ground chicken thigh
1 T. dried oregano
1 t. garlic powder
1 t. sea salt
¼ c. crushed Enjoy Life Foods Garlic and Parmesan Lentil Chips (alternatively you can use your favorite allergy friendly breadcrumb)
½ c. shredded mozzarella cheese*

Directions
1. Preheat oven to 375 and line a baking sheet with parchment paper. Set aside.

2. Boil about 2 cups of water and pour over the sundried tomatoes to rehydrate. Let soak in the water about 10-20 minutes. Chop up in a mini food processor.

3. In a large bowl mix together all the ingredients with your hands until well blended.

4. Scoop out 12 meatballs on the parchment. Then lightly drizzle with olive oil and form into shaped balls.

5. Bake at 375 for 18 minutes. Serve with your favorite tomato sauce.

*TO MAKE DAIRY FREE: Use your favorite allergy friendly mozzarella shreds or simply eliminate and add 1 T.nutritional yeast!

HAPPY HELPS: I love to use Enjoy Life Foods Garlic and Parmesan Lentil Chips as breadcrumbs. They are already flavored and crush beautifully so you have an allergy free one for one substitute for breadcrumbs that is delicious.

LETTUCE WRAPS

I began making these as part of a detox menu for clients. They loved them so much that they are now on regular rotation not only in my clients homes but also in my own! They're super fun for kids because it's like a "Choose Your Own Adventure" book, they can assemble their own wrap and take ownership of their food. You know kids love that!

Ingredients

1 lb. ground chicken thigh
4 green onions, finely minced
2" ginger, peeled and grated
1 garlic clove, grated
¼ c. minced cilantro
1 t. coriander powder
2 t. cumin powder
1 t. curry powder
1 t. sea salt
1 head butter lettuce, leaves cleaned and separated
vegetable options for assembly: 2 baby cucumbers (thinly sliced), mint leaves, cilantro leaves, microgreens, sliced avocado, sliced red pepper
Dipping sauce options
3 T. fish sauce + 3 T. lime juice + 1 T. coconut sugar
prepared sweet and sour sauce
¼ c. coconut aminos + 1 minced green onion + 1" ginger peeled and grated

Directions

1. In a large bowl mix together the ground chicken thigh, minced green onions, grated ginger, grated garlic, minced cilantro, coriander, cumin, curry powder and sea salt.

2. Preheat a medium saute pan. Add a drizzle of oil and wait another 30 seconds until hot. Add in the chicken mixture and cook, breaking apart with a spoon, until the mixture is cooked through and lightly golden.

3. Pour cooked chicken mixture into a bowl and serve alongside the lettuce leaves, vegetables and dipping sauces to allow everyone to make their own lettuce wraps!

Happy Helps: To make this vegan simply eliminate the chicken thigh and substitute cooked beluga lentils or quinoa. They'll both pick up the seasoning just like the chicken and work beautifully in a lettuce wrap.

WHIPPED HUMMUS

This is one of my favorite things to stock my clients fridges with. When the kids come home from school I like to lay out lots of cut vegetables, guacamole and this hummus. You'd be surprised how they grab and eat without any resistance or whining for chips or gummy snacks. Also one of my favorite spreads for a sandwhich or as a "dressing" for Buddha bowls!

Ingredients
1-15 oz. can of chickpeas, rinsed
juice of 1 lemon
1 peeled garlic clove
2 T. olive oil
2-3 T. tahini
2-3 T. water
sea salt
Optional add ins: black pepper and turmeric, ½ roasted red pepper, 1 cup spinach, 1 T. curry powder, chopped fresh herbs

Directions
1. Pour everything into the bowl of a food processor and blend until nice and smooth, about 3-4 minutes. Add salt to taste.

2. Add more water, olive oil or tahini as needed to thin to the desired consistency. I like my hummus pretty thick but creamy and whipped so I like to leave the processor on for a few minutes to really fluff it up!

POWER BITES

Ingredients

1 ¼ c. whole almonds, roasted and salted*
1 ¾ c. walnuts, raw*
½ c. whole gluten free oats
4 medjool dates, pitted
1 banana
3 T. coconut manna*
6 T. maple syrup
2 T. chia seeds
1 T. hemp seeds
1 t. vanilla extract
½ t. ground cinnamon
½ c. mini chocolate chips
Optional add ins: ashwagandha powder, reishi powder, collagen

Directions

1. Line a baking sheet with parchment paper and set aside.

2. Place everything except the mini chocolate chips in the bowl of a food processor and blend, scraping down sides occasionally, until everything is mixed together and you have a well blended mixture (add in any optionals if you are adding those now).

3. Scrape into a bowl and mix in the mini chocolate chips by hand.

4. Form into the size of a golf ball and roll. Place on parchment lined sheet and place in refrigerator to harden for about an hour.

5. Pop into a resealable container and keep in the refrigerator for handy snacking!

*TO MAKE TREE NUT FREE: Substitute pumpkin seeds for the almonds, sunflower seeds for the walnuts and sunflower seed butter for the coconut manna.

HAPPY HELPS: Be sure you use a large food processor for this recipe. The miniature version sadly isn't strong enough to work here and a blender just won't cut it. Also, if you have anything smaller than a 14 cup workbowl it will work best to prepare in two batches.

HAPPY PANTRY GLOSSARY

Here are some of the more unique ingredients that I commonly stock in my pantry. Many of my recipes have optional add-ins of these ingredients depending on what you feel your body might need. Of course, talking with your doctor, naturopath, acupuncturist is always a good idea. You can find my "special ingredients" listed here along with their health benefits. I find the following company's websites helpful in sourcing these specialty ingredients: Vitacost, Enjoy Life Foods, Sun Warrior and Moon Juice.

Ashwaganda - Is typically a powder that originates from a shrub. It is very common in Ayurvedic medicine and is believed to help with stress, difficulty concentrating, lack of energy and fatigue. You may also see it referred to as an adaptogen (a combination of amino acids, vitamins and herbs), meaning it adapts to what the body needs from internal as well as external stresses and helps heal it in that manner.

Bee Pollen - Little pellets of, you guessed it, pollen collected from bees. Bee pollen is known to be a nutrient powerhouse consisting of 18 vitamins including B-Complex and all amino acids. A simple little sprinkle into your cereal or over your smoothie is a great way to add it into your routine. It can help with beauty (increase blood supply to skin cells), circulation (strengthen blood vessel walls) and allergies (collected from local flowers, helps your body build up resistance).

Cacao Nibs - I love love love love the tangy bite of cacao nibs. All they are: crushed up, unsweetened cocoa beans. They have a gorgeous chocolate flavor with the benefits of fiber, iron, magnesium and loads of antioxidants. Add them to yogurt, top a smoothie with them, drizzle a banana with almond butter and cacao nibs….get crazy!

Chia Seeds - These cute little guys are an easy way to add omega-3 fatty acids to your diet. It's important to have a balance of omega 3, 6 and 9 (too much 6 and 9 can thicken your arterial walls, the 3 helps balance that out and keep blood flowing freely). They can absorb a ton of liquid and are a great way to thicken smoothies. You can also make an allergy free egg for baking with 1 T. chia seeds and 3 T. hot water!

Chlorella Liquid - This super green liquid, derived usually from algae, is known for its detoxifying and immune benefits. An easy add to any smoothie or even yogurt! Research has shown potential to bind to heavy metals in the body and help remove them from the body.

Coconut Manna - One of my favorite things ever!! It's just pureed coconut meat but has a naturally sweet flavor and is chock full of healthy fats to help keep you full and happy!